FOUR STEPS TO EFFECTIVE NEGOTIATIONS

LEARN NEGOTIATION SKILLS IN FOUR EASY STEPS

RON KEARN

Copyright © 2021 by Ronald Kearn, All rights reserved.

No part of this work may be used, reproduced or transmitted in whole or in part in any form or by any means, electronic or mechanical, including photocopying, scanning, recording, uploading, downloading or the use of any information storage and retrieval system, without prior written permission from the publisher.

For further information, visit:

www.winnoracademyofbusinessenglish.com

ron@winnoracademyofbusinessenglish.com

Contents

Introduction 5
   What is negotiation? 6
   Negotiator 8
   Negotiator's skills 9
   Negotiation Elements 10
MODELS OF NEGOTIATION 11
   Win-Win Model 12
   Win-Lose Model 13
   The Lose-Lose Model 14
      Case 1 15
      Case 2 15
      Case 3 16
   4. RADPAC Model of Negotiation 16
Types of Negotiation inCorporates 20
Role of Personality in Negotiation 26
   Individuals must strive to be themselves during negotiations. 26
   It is critical to be sincere rather than merely serious. 27
Negotiating for Success: Basic Phase 32
Preparation Phase 34
      What Do I Want? 35

    What is my backup plan if we are unable to reach an agreement? 37

    Calculate the Value of Your Reservation 38

    Evaluate Your Counterpart's BATNA 39

Exchange Information and Discussion Phase 40

Bargaining Phase 43

Closing and Commitment Phase 46

Summary 49

INTRODUCTION

Let us begin by examining a real-world scenario to gain a better understanding of negotiation.

Your friends have invited you to join them for a late-night movie. However, you are well aware that your parents will never appreciate your staying away from home late at night, and you certainly don't want to miss the movie or your friends' company.

What would you do in this situation? Will you engage in combat with everyone?

Another circumstance

After a full day of shopping, Tom visited a nearby mall and came across a CD player he immediately liked. The CD player cost around $30, but he was unfortunately short on cash. He couldn't leave the CD player because it was an exclusive model, and Tom had been eyeing it for quite some time.

In such a situation, what would Tom do?

All of the above questions can be answered with a single word: "Negotiation." You negotiate to achieve your objectives without fear of conflict or misunderstanding. It is a peaceful method of completing tasks without provoking anyone's wrath.

We can all agree that no one has ever benefited from conflict or disagreement. Disputes exacerbate our stress, and we are perpetually restless. One loses focus, and his interest in the organization dwindles over time. It is always prudent to consult with one another and negotiate a beneficial solution to all negotiations.

What is negotiation?

Negotiation is a technique for debating issues among one's peers and reaching an agreement that benefits all parties involved. It is a highly effective method of avoiding conflicts and tensions. When individuals disagree, they convene, discuss issues in an open forum, negotiate with one another, and arrive at an acceptable solution. In layman's terms, this is also referred to as bargaining.

Please review the preceding two real-world scenarios.

You wish to go to the movies but know your parents would never let you. Are you going to quarrel with your parents? Obviously, no, you will sit with them and do your best to persuade and negotiate with them without engaging in combat and ruining everyone's mood. Probably, you'll spend the upcoming weekend with your parents if they agree to your going to the movie today; otherwise, you'll negotiate with your friends to get a noon show. Negotiation enables you to accomplish your objective without causing harm to anyone. In this case, your objective is to attend a movie, which you negotiate with your parents or friends.

In the second situation, Tom cannot afford to lose the CD player due to its exclusivity, and thus attempts to negotiate a lower price with the store owner to benefit both parties.

Negotiation is crucial in both business and personal life to maintain peace and happiness.

Your boss requests that you submit a report within two working days, although the report is somewhat critical and requires additional time. Will you agree to your boss's request solely to appease him? Your yes may make the boss happy at the time, but if you fail to submit it within the specified time frame, you will find yourself in serious trouble. It's often advisable to bargain with your boss rather than accept something you know is difficult. Solicit additional time from your boss or, more likely, avoid producing an exhaustive report. Negotiation is preferable because it avoids sullying your relationship with your superiors later.

Negotiator

A negotiator is a person who represents an organization or a position and carefully listens to all parties to reach an agreement that is willingly acceptable to all.

Negotiator's skills

A negotiator should ideally be objective and neutral, with no preference for any party.

He needs to understand the situation and the parties involved to make a decision that benefits everyone.

People are not always willing to accept the negotiator's decision; they may object if they believe their interests are not met. When a negotiator is left with no choice, he must use his power to impose his ideas on everyone; after all, one cannot please everyone.

A negotiator must be tactful and intelligent enough to handle all possible situations and reach a conclusion.

Negotiation Elements

Negotiation

↓

Process + Behaviour + Substance (Agenda)

- ❖ **Process:** The process of negotiation refers to how individuals negotiate with one another. The procedure encompasses the various techniques and strategies used to negotiate and come to an agreement.
- ❖ **Behavior:** The way two parties interact with one another during the negotiation process is referred to as their behavior. The way they interact with one another and communicate with one another to make their points clear all fall under the category of behavior.
- ❖ **Substance:** Individuals must have a plan upon which to negotiate. A subject is critical for negotiation. In the first scenario, going to a late-night movie was the point of contention between you and your parents and friends.

MODELS OF NEGOTIATION

Negotiation is defined as a discussion between individuals to reach an agreement that is acceptable to all parties. It is a process in which people, rather than fighting, sit down together, weigh the pros and cons, and then come up with a solution that benefits everyone.

When Sam wanted to purchase a mobile phone, he made every effort to purchase it at the lowest possible price, and the shopkeeper made sure he earned his profit as well. Thus, the negotiation benefited Sam, as he avoided paying large sums of money, and the shopkeeper, as he earned his profits.

Negotiation assists in resolving conflicts and disagreements between individuals. Negotiation is necessary for all aspects of life to ensure a peaceful and stress-free existence.

Let us examine various negotiation models:

Win-Win Model

In this model, every party to the negotiation wins. Nobody loses in this model, and everyone gains from the negotiation. It is the most widely accepted negotiation model.

Allow me to illustrate with an example:

Daniel desired to purchase a laptop, but the model was prohibitively expensive. He went to the outlet and negotiated a lower price with the shopkeeper. The shopkeeper was initially hesitant, but he quoted a price acceptable to both parties after several rounds of discussion and persuasion. Daniel was delighted because he could now afford the laptop without burning a hole in his pocket. The negotiation benefited the store owner as well, as he was able to earn profits and gained a loyal customer who would return in the future.

Win-Lose Model

This model results in one party winning and the other party losing. In this model, one party benefits while the other party remains dissatisfied after several rounds of discussions and negotiations.

Please refer to the preceding example, in which Daniel desired to purchase a laptop. In this case, both Daniel and the store owner benefited from the transaction. Assume Daniel cannot afford the storeowner's quoted price and requests that he reduce it further. Suppose the store owner continues to reduce the price. In that case, he will be unable to earn a profit, but Daniel will be extremely happy. Thus, Daniel would be satisfied following the negotiation, but the shopkeeper would not. In a win-lose scenario, neither of the two parties is satisfied. Only one of the parties walks away with a benefit.

The Lose-Lose Model

As the name implies, this model assumes that the negotiation outcome is zero. This model benefits no one.

Daniel would not have gotten anything out of the deal if he had not purchased the laptop following several negotiation rounds. Daniel would return empty-handed, implying that the store owner would earn nothing.

In this model, the two parties are generally unwilling to accept one another's viewpoints and are opposed to compromising. No discussions are beneficial.

Let us illustrate the three models above with a case study from the corporate world.

Mike was chosen to work for a reputable multinational corporation. He was summoned to negotiate his salary with Sara, the organization's human resources director.

Case 1

Sara proposed a salary to Mike, but Mike was unimpressed. He insisted Sara increase his salary as much as possible. Sara arrived at a figure acceptable to Mike following discussions, and she immediately released his offer letter. Mike landed his dream job, and Sara offered Mike a salary that perfectly fits the company's budget. A Situation in Which Everyone Benefits (Both the parties gained)

Case 2

Sara's superior negotiation skills convinced Mike to accept a slightly lower salary than he quoted. Mike wanted to seize the opportunity as well, as it was his dream job, which he had been eyeing for quite some time. He was forced to accept an offer with a slightly lower salary than anticipated. Thus, Mike was not completely satisfied with this negotiation, but Sara was - a win-lose negotiation.

Case 3

Mike declined the offer because Sara's salary quote fell short of his expectations. Sara made every effort to reason with Mike, but it was fruitless. - A lose-lose negotiation model. Nobody benefited from this negotiation, neither Mike nor Sara.

4. RADPAC Model of Negotiation

The RADPAC Model of Negotiation is a widely used negotiation model in business.

Let us examine it in greater detail.

Each letter in this model represents something:

R - Rapport

A - Analysis

D - Debate

P - Propose

A - Agreement

C - Close

R - Rapport: As the name implies, this term refers to the relationship between the parties to a negotiation. The parties to negotiation should ideally be at ease with one another and have a positive rapport.

A - Analysis: One party must have a thorough understanding of the other. Individuals must understand one another's needs and interests. While the shopkeeper must understand the customer's needs and budget, the customer must not overlook the shopkeeper's profits. Individuals must pay close attention to one another.

D - Debate: Nothing is possible without discussion. This round entails a discussion of issues between the parties to the negotiation. This round weighs the advantages and disadvantages of an idea. Individuals argue with one another, and each attempts to persuade the other. One must not lose his temper during this round but must maintain his composure and composure.

P - Propose: In this round, each participant submits his or her best idea. Each person makes every effort to come up with the best possible idea and reach an acceptable agreement.

A - Agreement: At this stage, individuals conclude and agree on the absolute best option.

C - Close: The negotiation is successful, and all parties are satisfied.

Consider Mike and Sara's example once more to gain a better understanding of the RADPAC Model.

R - Mike and Sara's rapport. They must be at ease with one another and should avoid initiating the negotiation immediately. To begin, they must break the ice. The conversations must begin with a friendly smile and greetings.

A - Mike and Sara would make every effort to understand one another needs. Mike's objective is to seize the opportunity; Sara's objective is to hire an employee for the organization.

D - Mike and Sara's various rounds of discussion. Mike and Sara would argue with one another in an attempt to obtain what they desired.

P - Mike would propose the highest salary he can earn. At the same time, Sara would also discuss the highest salary her company is capable of offering.

A - Mike and Sara would make every effort to understand one another needs.

C - The negotiation has concluded. The next course of action has been determined; in this case, the next step would be the generation and acceptance of the offer letter.

TYPES OF NEGOTIATION INCORPORATES

Negotiation is the process by which individuals communicate to reach a mutually beneficial agreement. Negotiation is how individuals weigh the advantages and disadvantages of a situation and reach an agreement that benefits everyone. Individuals make every effort during negotiation to reach an agreement that is acceptable to all parties. In simpler terms, it is referred to as bartering.

Corporates negotiate in a variety of ways to increase output and improve employee relations.

Let us take a closer look at the different types of negotiation:

- **Daily Negotiation at Workplace:** Daily, we negotiate something or other at work, either with our superiors or with our coworkers, to ensure that work runs smoothly. These are referred to as "day-to-day negotiations."

- **Employee-supervisor-negotiation:** A workplace; an employee must negotiate with their superiors to ensure that they are assigned responsibilities aligned with their interests and specialization. Accept nothing that makes you uneasy. Discuss your concerns with your boss. Suppose your boss has asked you to prepare a report on the organization's branding and marketing strategies, even though marketing has never been your area of expertise. Accept it only if your boss directs you to. Negotiate with him; you may be able to cover another subject and have someone else prepare the report on marketing and branding. It is preferable to negotiate in the beginning to avoid future conflicts and misunderstandings. Before accepting any offer, an individual should negotiate his salary with the prospective employer to avoid future conflict. If you are not receiving what you deserve, your work will never be enjoyable. Accepting any offer simply because you require work is never a good idea; it is always prudent to negotiate well before joining any organization.

- **Negotiation between colleagues:** Negotiation between team members is critical for reducing the likelihood of disagreements and conflicts. An anyone team member should not be overburdened while the rest of the team relaxes. One should bargain with his coworkers and accept only those responsibilities for which he believes he is capable. The burden of achieving the targets should not fall on a single shoulder but should be evenly distributed among all. Negotiate with your team members and willingly accept new responsibilities. If you wish to take a few days off, arrange for a team member to cover your work in your absence. When he takes a leave of absence, you can assist him in the same manner.

Negotiation contributes to the team's output and, ultimately, the organization's productivity. Because people achieve what they expect, misunderstandings and conflicts are significantly reduced, and the office becomes a more pleasant place to work.

- **Commercial negotiations:** Generally, commercial negotiations take the form of contracts. Two parties sit across the table from one another, discuss issues, and agree on both parties' acceptable terms. In such instances, everything should be crystal clear. Both parties sign a contract and agree to abide by its terms and conditions.

Cherry was representing a reputable organization's administration department. He was tasked with the responsibility of procuring bulk laptops from a vendor for the office's employees. He requested a price quotation from the vendor. Cherry determined that the price was out of line with the company's budget. Thus, he sat down with the vendor and negotiated the price with him. Eventually, both parties agreed on a price that was acceptable to both parties. Cherry and the vendor signed a contract outlining the payment terms, payment mode, delivery date, warranty information, and other critical terms and conditions. Commercial negotiations almost always involve an outside party. Thus a contract is necessary to ensure that no party withdraws later.

- **Legal Negotiation:** Legal negotiation occurs between an individual and the law. The individual is required to follow the rules and regulations established by the legal system. At the same time, the legal system also takes into account the individual's needs and interests.

Negotiations are critical in the workplace to ensure that everyone is satisfied and that no one feels excluded or overlooked. Additionally, it alleviates conflicts and misunderstandings among coworkers.

ROLE OF PERSONALITY IN NEGOTIATION

For an effective negotiation, an imposing personality must coexist with effective communication. **Effective negotiation requires a charming personality.**

Let us examine how one's personal traits contribute to effective negotiation.

Individuals must strive to be themselves during negotiations.

One should not deceive others or pretend to be something they are not. If you are not satisfied with the transaction, do not pretend to be. It is preferable to express a concern immediately rather than later. Maintain a normal state of mind and relaxation; things will naturally fall into place.

It is critical to be sincere rather than merely serious.

Sincerity is a critical personality trait for negotiation. Effective negotiation requires sincerity. Take nothing for granted. Prepare thoroughly for your negotiation for a business transaction and attempt to research all aspects of the transaction in advance thoroughly. The negotiation's plan must be crystal clear to you. Carry all pertinent documents that you may require during the negotiation. Don't go for the sake of going.

Be truthful: Falsify nothing. Honesty is critical during negotiations. Never manipulate one's salary to obtain a raise in the next organization. Speak no untruths for the sake of money. Fear of being apprehended would always be present, and it would reflect on your face as well. Do not be concerned; you will undoubtedly receive what you deserve.

If you know the laptop will cost you XYZ, do not go to the shopkeeper and claim it is significantly cheaper in the next shop. He is not a bumbling businessman. Bear in mind that he, too, keeps an eye on the prices offered by his fellow shopkeepers. It is preferable to request discounts or possibly additional accessories rather than lower the price, which you know is difficult for the shopkeeper.

One should dress very well for a negotiation: Our clothing has a significant impact on how our personality is enhanced. A person who is dressed shabbily will have a difficult time convincing the other person.

Bear in mind that the first impression is the lasting impression, and thus one must exercise extreme caution.

Consider how you will feel interacting with a shopkeeper who is not dressed impeccably, has a very casual demeanor, and is nearly half asleep. You will not bother to listen to him at all.

Jack wore a t-shirt and jeans to a business meeting. The other party assumed that Jack was not serious about the transaction and showed little interest in the negotiations. The smart dressing does not mean dressing extravagantly; rather, it means dressing appropriately for the occasion. For business meetings, prefer formal attire, and don't forget to polish your shoes for maximum impact. People do take notice of your shoes.

Be Patient: Impatient individuals have been observed to be poor negotiators. Do not believe that if you request that an item's price be $4, the shopkeeper will immediately agree and gladly give it to you. You must persuade him, which requires patience. You are not permitted to lose your temper and yell at him.

Be adaptable and encourage yourself to compromise: It is acceptable to prioritize one's personal interests, but one should not be self-centered. If you are the first to accept something, you will not lose significance or gain anything; rather, the other person will look up to you, and both of you will gain whatever you desire.

To conduct a more effective negotiation, one must trust the second party: Do not constantly look for faults in others. Not everyone is evil; some people are genuinely kind and helpful. One should not always assume the other person intends to cause him harm. The second party is present solely to conduct business; he is in no way your adversary. Instead of getting straight to the point, begin the conversation with a warm smile. Take the initiative to compliment him if he is wearing a nice shirt. Consider him a friend. Never be arrogant. He, like you, is representing his company. Place an order for coffee and snacks. It will aid in breaking the ice and fortifying the two parties' bond. Bear in mind that one should not be excessively casual or friendly.

Maintain a professional approach: Once your transaction is complete, both parties should sign a contract in their presence. To ensure greater clarity, the minutes of the meeting must be distributed to all participants. Remember to collect your bills from the shopkeeper once you're finished shopping. Rely on nonverbal communication as well.

Improve your listening skills in order to conduct a more effective negotiation: Additionally, listen to the opposing party. He may come up with something interesting that is also beneficial to you. Do not assume that the other person is ignorant; he, too, has arrived well prepared. Never underestimate the opposing party. When shopping, do not disregard the shopkeeper; instead, listen to him and then decide what to purchase and what not to.

Be a little diplomatic and tactful: Being diplomatic does not imply intelligence. Between the two, there is a difference. One must be intelligent and know when and when not to speak. Analyze the situation and act appropriately. Avoid speaking something simply because your boss has requested that you do so. Utilize your intellect and react appropriately. If you believe your statements will come across as foolish in a particular situation, it is better to remain silent.

NEGOTIATING FOR SUCCESS: BASIC PHASE

Each individual engages in negotiation. We bargain with family members over how to spend vacation time;

we bargain with friends over who pays for dinner; and we bargain with contractors over when to come to the house for a delivery or repair. Physicians negotiate with patients when it comes to medical versus surgical therapy or, more often than not, no therapy at all. Scientists bargain for experimentation time and space. We all bargain for our salaries and job responsibilities. While each of these examples presents a unique set of risks and consequences, they all require basic communication skills to be effective.

Richard Shell defines negotiation as an interactive communication process that occurs whenever we want something from another person or another person wants something from us in his book, Bargaining for Advantage (Penguin Books 1999). Shell divides the process into four Phase:

- ❖ Preparation
- ❖ Exchange Information and Discussion
- ❖ Bargaining
- ❖ Closing and Commitment

The four phases are discussed in detail in this book using examples from everyday interactions between faculty members negotiating new positions in business schools.

PREPARATION PHASE

A good negotiation preparation process entails devoting sufficient time to considering what we want, the alternatives to the current deal, and our counterpart's potential value.

When a critical negotiation looms, winging it is never an option. The most skilled negotiators conduct extensive negotiation preparation. It requires ample time to analyze your objectives, your bargaining position, and the other side's likely objectives and alternatives.

Leigh Thompson of Northwestern University recommends that negotiators conduct a thorough self-assessment before negotiating in her book The Mind and Heart of the Negotiator. She recommends, in particular, that you ask two primary questions as part of your negotiation preparation:

1. What do I want?
2. What is my backup plan if we are unable to reach an agreement?

What Do I Want?

Thompson's first question necessitates that we establish an ambitious but attainable goal. Thompson notes three traps to avoid when setting a target.

To begin, avoid being an inexperienced negotiator who sets an unrealistic target. If you do, you risk becoming a victim of the "winner's curse," which refers to the disappointment we experience when the other party accepts our initial offer in a negotiation. The fact that the other party is eager to accept your initial offer indicates that you set your sights too low and did not conduct adequate preparation for the negotiation.

However, you do not want to be an overly ambitious negotiator. When you set your sights too high and refuse to make substantial concessions, you will find yourself without a deal.

A third issue arises when you have done so little preparation for the negotiation that you are unsure of what you want. Negotiators frequently regard the other party's good faith proposals with suspicion or disappointment in this case.

What is my backup plan if we are unable to reach an agreement?

To increase your chances of meeting a realistic but ambitious goal, you must first identify your best alternative to a negotiated agreement, or **BATNA**, (Best Alternative To a Negotiated Agreement) as Roger Fisher, William Ury, and Bruce Patton recommend in Getting to Yes: Negotiating Agreement Without Giving In.

Determining your BATNA will help you determine when to abandon the project and pursue your best alternative. Professors Deepak Malhotra and Max H. Bazerman of Harvard Business School note in their book Negotiation Genius that BATNA assessment entails the following three steps:

1. Make a list of all viable alternatives you might pursue if you cannot agree with the current party.
2. Calculate the value of each alternative.
3. Determine the best alternative, referred to as your BATNA.

For a job seeker who is preparing for a specific hiring negotiation, the first step would be to identify alternative job opportunities and other options, such as remaining at her current job or applying to graduate school. The second step would be to evaluate each alternative's monetary and non-monetary value, including anticipated salary, benefits, responsibilities, engagement with one's work, and overall quality of life. This type of analysis should help the job seeker identify her preferred alternative.

Calculate the Value of Your Reservation

Once you've identified your BATNA through negotiation preparation, you can calculate your reservation value, or reservation price, which is your walk-away point in the upcoming negotiation. It could be a specific number in a price negotiation. In an integrative negotiation involving multiple issues, your reservation value may be expressed as a package, such as the lowest salary, benefits, and responsibilities you would accept in exchange for taking a particular job.

Knowing the value of your reservation will assist you in avoiding two errors:

1) accepting a deal that is worse than your BATNA
2) rejecting a deal that is better than your BATNA.

Evaluate Your Counterpart's BATNA

When preparing for a negotiation, it is insufficient to focus exclusively on one's own needs and desires. To increase the likelihood of a mutually beneficial deal, you must also ascertain the other party's willingness to give. To do so, you must conduct a BATNA analysis.

Consider the following: "What will they do if our negotiation comes to a stalemate?" It prompts you to consider the other party's reservation value. For example, a job seeker may conclude that the hiring organization has other qualified candidates waiting to take the job at a low salary. If this is the case, the job seeker may recognize that he will have little leverage over the hiring manager during a salary negotiation. On the other hand, a job seeker may be aware that she is one of the few qualified candidates for an open position—in which case, she may negotiate a favorable deal.

Negotiation preparation must begin with an objective assessment of the playing field. The more rational and systematic your negotiation preparation process, the more favorable the outcome of your negotiations.

EXCHANGE INFORMATION AND DISCUSSION PHASE

It is the most critical stage of the negotiation process. In 1978, a study of English labor and contract negotiators conducting actual transactions revealed that successful negotiators asked twice as many questions and spent more than twice as much time acquiring and clarifying information as average negotiators.

Negotiating behavior	Skilled	Average
Questions, as % of all negotiating behavior	21.3	9.6
Active listening: Testing for understanding	9.7	4.1
Active listening: Summarizing	7.5	4.2
Total information exchange	38.5	17.9

Since 1978, numerous observational studies have confirmed the critical nature of these fundamental communication skills in effective negotiation. Henry Ford advised on such communication: "If there is one secret to success," he said, "it is the ability to see things from the other person's perspective as well as your own." Why are interpersonal communication skills critical in this type of interaction? Shell speculates, "Most people are so appreciative of having an attentive audience that they ignore your tactful probing until they feel compelled to obtain a few answers themselves." By that time, the effective negotiator has gathered the information necessary to frame precisely the correct responses."

Dr. Timothy Johnson interviewed various decision-makers within the department and medical school during his search for the position of chair of obstetrics and gynecology at the University of Michigan. The conversations and contemplation of what might be possible to build in the medical school resulted in an 18-page vision and planning document. This document reflected the department's and medical school's visions and possibilities. It required little negotiation to reach an agreement due to the shared interests and common ground shared by those with whom he would ultimately develop the vision. And how did he discover common interests and the possibility of establishing a great department? By inquiring, listening, elucidating, and cultivating shared interests.

BARGAINING PHASE

Bargaining is the stage of negotiation that the majority of people associate with it. However, this stage is NOT a stage of negotiation in and of itself. It begins with a discussion of terms, with the initiation of the discussion of a "deal." Dr. Steve Blum instructs AAMC EDS participants to postpone this stage as long as possible and recognize when it occurs. "As soon as a number or term is mentioned by one party, you have shifted from information exchange to bargaining," he teaches. In well-managed negotiations that have progressed successfully through the stage of information exchange, this transition occurs naturally as a natural extension of how to implement the emerging ideas. If the exchange is conducted effectively, both parties are likely to have discovered a variety of alternative resolutions that are more appealing than the initial ideas brought to the discussion by either party.

Additionally, both parties are more likely to be satisfied with the final transaction if they approach the discussion with the best-case scenario in mind. The adage "think positive" is appropriate in negotiations. According to legend, King Ching of Chou stated in the 12th century, "High achievement results from lofty goals." Consider meeting mutual needs and desires through complementary solutions when negotiating. Naturally, one must be well prepared by understanding the bottom line or Best Alternative to a Negotiated Agreement. (We will discuss BATNA in greater detail in a subsequent issue.) And, of course, it is critical to understand one's values to avoid compromising them. On the other hand, the best bargaining will leave all parties feeling like they gained something and lost little or nothing. When sufficient time is spent before the bargaining stage, it occurs to establish common ground on values and mutual benefit in exchanging property or ideas.

The significant curriculum changes implemented across the country result from effective negotiation with diverse individuals with diverse interests. The "bargain" is frequently used to increase one department's visibility in exchange for support for more dispersed or integrated teaching. Often, this entails negotiating a new method of allocating funds to departments to recognize teaching effort while also considering the impact of these new distribution methods on departmental and divisional budgeting. Each of these outcomes is the result of a bargaining process that contributes to a broader vision of more effective teaching, learning, and organizational innovation

CLOSING AND COMMITMENT PHASE

Negotiations require closure. After a negotiation, you and the other party will have reached an agreement on the terms, or one party will have determined that the final offer is unacceptable and must be withdrawn. The majority of negotiators believe that if their best offer is rejected, there is nothing else they can do. You made the best offer you could, and that is all you can do. However, the most astute negotiators view rejection as an opportunity to grow. "How long would it have taken for us to agree?"

A CEO was recently negotiating with a customer. When the CEO learned the customer had chosen the competition, he decided to inquire why negotiations had broken down. With nothing to lose, the CEO called the prospect's vice president and inquired why the offer was rejected, explaining that the information would be used to improve future offerings. Surprisingly, the VP explained that the competitor received the deal because, despite charging more, the competitor provided after-sales support for the product. The CEO was taken aback, initially assuming that the VP's primary objective was to obtain the lowest possible price. To achieve such a low price, various extras such as after-sales service were eliminated from the offer. After learning that the VP was looking for service, not the lowest price, the CEO stated, "Now that I know what I know now, I'm confident that I could have outbid the competitor." Are you willing to accept a revised offer?" The VP agreed, and the CEO received a signed contract a week later. D. Malhotra & M. H. Bazerman (2007, September). Harvard Business Review, 85, p. 72.

Occasionally, after negotiations, it becomes clear why a deal was not reached. However, if you're unsure why a deal fell through, consider making a follow-up call. Even if you do not reclaim the deal, you may learn something useful for future negotiations. Additionally, the other party may be more receptive to disclosing information if they believe you are not in a "selling" mode.

SUMMARY

The most effective way to increase your negotiation effectiveness is to be aware of your opportunities and work on them consciously. Blum credits Shell with instilling in him the belief that effective negotiators share specific characteristics. They are all:

- ❖ plan and prepare systematically
- ❖ have high goals
- ❖ continue to uphold a reputation for reliability and integrity

demonstrate superior listening abilities, subject matter knowledge, verbal abilities, and self-confidence.

Fortunately, all of these characteristics are also necessary for academic success. Whether your primary focus is clinical care, educational innovation, or scientific research, you have most likely developed a strong foundation in each of these abilities and characteristics. Using the four stages, you should be able to increase the effectiveness of your negotiations. Drs. Jayne Thorson, Tim Johnson, and Dee Fenner of the University of Michigan College of Medicine shared some basic tips for negotiating new academic positions at the 2004 AAMC Annual Meeting. All of these rely on the fundamental stages of negotiation, which Dr. Fenner refers to as "a universal dance with four steps."